T0097030

THE *Aunties*
KEEPSAKE BOOK

ALSO BY TAMARA TRAEDER & JULIENNE BENNETT:

Aunties: Our Older, Cooler, Wiser Friends
(Wildcat Canyon Press, 1998)

OTHER BOOKS BY TAMARA TRAEDER:

girlfriends Talk About Men: Sharing Secrets for a Great Relationship
(with Carmen Renee Berry, Wildcat Canyon Press, 1997)

The girlfriends Keepsake Book: The Story of Our Friendship
(with Carmen Renee Berry, Wildcat Canyon Press, 1996)

girlfriends: Invisible Bonds, Enduring Ties
(with Carmen Renee Berry, Wildcat Canyon Press, 1996)

ALSO BY JULIENNE BENNETT:

Where the Heart Is: A Celebration of Home
(co-edited with Mimi Luebbermann, Wildcat Canyon Press, 1995)

THE *Aunties*
KEEPSAKE BOOK
The Story of Our Friendship

TAMARA TRAEDER AND
JULIENNE BENNETT

WILDCAT CANYON PRESS
A Division of Circulus Publishing Group, Inc.
Berkeley, California

Editor: Roy M. Carlisle
Copyeditor: Jean Blomquist
Cover and Interior Design: Gordon Chun Design
Typographic Specifications: Text: Novarese Book; Titles: Novarese Medium

Printed in Canada

Distributed to the trade by Publishers Group West
10 9 8 7 6 5 4 3 2 1

THE AUNTIE CONNECTION

*F*or as long as there have been women, there have been aunties. Aunties have always been crucial in their roles as our "other mothers"—those other women who helped raise us. But they are even more important to us now. As parents separate, as extended families become more physically distant, aunties are needed more than ever.

Many of us who have aunties, or who are aunties, know that a blood relationship is not necessary in order to fill this role. Even if a woman does not have a sibling with children, aunts and nieces can be found among and adopted from the rest of the population. A female child of a neighbor, a student, a young person met in an organization such as Big Brothers/Big Sisters, can be a potential niece. Many women consider one or more of their mother's friends to be their closest aunties.

We may not actually call this woman "Auntie" or even "Aunt." Auntie is more a role than a moniker. An auntie is someone who is older, interested, a good listener, and a helpful adviser. She may also be someone who seems glamorous, or simply lives a very different life than our own mother does and provides another example of who we can be as women. Especially when we were young, aunties may simply have been the women with whom we had an enormous amount of fun, with whom we treasured spending time.

Aunts are important in the lives of young men as well as young women, but we have found that aunties and nieces, whether blood-related or connected by an honorary relationship, often have been more intensely affected by each other. Many women speak of how their aunties greatly influenced who they were to become as adults. They were fascinated by their aunt's way of being in the world. Aunts often speak of how honored they are to have some influence on a growing girl, how seriously they take the relationship, and the importance of having a young woman in their lives. As Nancy tells us, "It is really exciting. I feel incredibly honored to have these kids in my life. They trust me to be a source for love, hugs, and advice. I love lending an ear to listen and just being a person who helps expand their worlds, just like mine was expanded by my auntie." Aunts cherish the fact that they play an important role in these younger women's lives, happily passing on their interests, attitudes, senses of humor, and even their educational paths or senses of style.

For women who do not have children of their own, these relationships often take on more significant overtones. A niece may be a daughter figure for a childless woman. The biological clock is not ticking, and a woman is never "too old" to be an auntie. One auntie points out that these relationships are becoming more important among the baby boomer generation. "Many people of my generation chose not to have children. I'm one of them. It didn't matter as much to me because I always had my relationship with my niece Lauren.

It has always felt like I was the mother generation and she was the daughter generation, and the fact that I was not her biological mother didn't really change that for me. So I always felt like I wasn't missing anything. We were as close as two human beings could ever be and we still are, so I think the fact that I didn't physically give birth to her didn't make that much difference."

Aunties need nieces, and nieces need aunties. It is never too late to find an aunt, or to be one! One of the extraordinary aspects of these relationships is that they are nonexclusive—one can have many aunties and many nieces. Girls and women profit from the influences of many women, who present different possibilities as to how we can live our lives as adults. The common characteristics of these relationships are our love for each other, our desire to spend time together, our respect for each other. These connections are about friendship, perhaps the first friendship, and the longest lasting, of our lives.

As we traveled around the country last year, talking to women about their aunties, we were struck by the number of stories that poured out of women—stories of adventure, stories of compassion, stories of deep friendship and respect between women of different generations. We hope that with this keepsake book, women who are lucky enough to have a valued auntie–and–niece relationship can record, for the sake of themselves and future generations of women, the love, memories, gratitude, and dreams they share.

This keepsake book is dedicated to the relationship

between _____, a fabulous auntie

and _____, a terrific niece.

PART ONE

OUR HISTORY

"I never before felt that kind of connection. It was like home.

Just like home. I can even remember where it was—

in the hallway of my apartment. I remember holding my niece up

and looking at her and feeling the full connection.

The feeling went really deep."

—Susie

I Remember When We Met

Sometimes we meet our aunties or our nieces when the niece is born, sometimes they come along later in our lives. Do you remember your first meeting?

We met when . . .

_____

_____

_____

The first thing I noticed about you was . . .

_____

The first thing you noticed about me was . . .

_____

I was _____ years old when we met and you were _____ years old.

Here is the earliest picture of us together:

I Found You a Friend

Patti, in her forties, tells us this story of meeting her aunt, "My aunt is not blood related, I literally found her. My parents and I had moved to Cincinnati, Ohio, from Indiana when I was about five or six years old. We lived in an apartment on a wonderful street and there was an alley where the kids would always come out and play. I would walk down the alley and see people— it was in the fifties so you could visit people and feel very comfortable. My mom was just starting to make friends like I was, and one day I saw this lovely woman down the street washing a white convertible. She had short black hair; a very, very pretty woman with a beautiful smile. She wore a white shirt and pants. I just went over and started talking to her. I felt totally drawn to her, I thought she was the neatest thing. So I went back to my mom and said, 'Mom, I found you a friend.' I remember dragging her down the alley, they met, and they have been best friends to this day."

BECOMING FRIENDS

*F*or many women, their aunties may have been their first adult friends, women they could talk to, who weren't their parents and who would introduce them to new experiences and interests. Sometimes a friendship is born when you least expect it. Write the story of how your relationship began.

_____

_____

_____

_____

_____

_____

_____

_____

_____

_____

A Thirst for Travel

Nancy B. recalls how she became friends with her sixth-grade teacher,
"When I was in sixth grade and eleven years old, I had a teacher named
Mary. She was great to everybody in the class, but we developed a special
friendship. I have nine brothers and sisters. My mom and dad were busy
people! There were things I received from Mary that I didn't get from my
own family, not because those things weren't there, it's just that there
wasn't time. She was the person in my life who was there with hugs and all
kinds of attention and affection. Mary taught me how to ski and play the
guitar; she taught me French. In sixth-grade geography, she instilled in me
an incredible interest in Europe and traveling. I remember vividly one day
after class pointing to Europe in my geography book and saying, 'One day,
I'm going to go there.' Mary said, 'I believe you will.' At eighteen years of
age, I did. It wasn't until after the fact that I realized that I went there,
because years earlier the seed had been planted and then it just grew and
grew. She broadened my horizons and made my world so much bigger.
As the years went on, we never lost contact. When Mary went to Europe,
I wrote her letters fervently. Today, I am forty years old, she is fifty-one,
and she remains one of my best friends."

SHE IS SO COOL

"**S**he is the most glamorous woman in the world" or similar sentiments are how nieces often describe their treasured aunties. "She is the sweetest, smartest young woman" is a statement we hear aunts make about the nieces with whom they have a close connection. If you were describing each other to a friend, what would you say?

The best characteristics of my aunt are . . .

_____

_____

_____

_____

_____

My niece is so cool because . . .

_____

_____

_____

_____

_____

Aunt Toots

Karen tells us about her Auntie Toots: "Her father nicknamed her Toots when she was a little girl because she was kind of roly-poly, like a Tootsie Roll. I just adored her. She and her daughter, Dawnie, lived with us growing up. Every weekend she used to take Dawnie and me, stand us at the bathroom mirror, and braid our hair so it wouldn't get snarled and messy when we sat in her red convertible to drive to the beach. Oh, she loved listening to fifties songs. We would listen to the oldies when we drove over Highway 17 from San Jose to Santa Cruz. My Auntie Toots and my cousin used to get these gorgeous tans, and I was so pale. I had sunblock on my nose and wore my hat, but I danced in the back seat with Dawnie anyway. My aunt would take us to Santa Cruz Boardwalk, buy us fried zucchini, and let us ride the bumper cars. She was a very dynamic person. We used to have a great time. Auntie Toots was very sensible, but to me she was the most exotic woman on earth. She used to dress in white miniskirts and white boots and drove convertibles. She was a real estate agent, so she was always meeting with clients. She didn't always have a lot of money, but somehow money was never an object."

*H*as anyone ever told you two that you seem like mother and daughter? Do you feel like you could be? Many times aunties and nieces find amazing similarities in their tastes, attitudes, or even their appearances. How are you alike?

_____

_____

_____

_____

_____

_____

_____

_____

"My mother had my niece Elaine's high school graduation picture out in her apartment and one of her friends came over. She laughed and asked her why she still had my graduation picture out. We are that identical."

—Jeannette

Taylor's Store

Susie laughingly tells us this story about her niece Taylor, "I'm an entrepreneur, so I am always working. I do public relations and events. Taylor created a little space out in the backyard for her 'store.' It was just a little area out in the trees, but Taylor roped it off and invited people to visit. She made some jewelry from her beads, picked wildflowers, put them in bottles and put a ribbon around them, and put them in her store. Folks would buy something from her for fifteen cents or whatever. The next time I visited her store it had expanded to the patio, which is pretty big. Everything was neatly lined up. She found old pots in the garage, three different sizes, and priced each one of them differently, like fifteen cents, twenty-five cents, seventy-five cents. She was hanging stuff on clotheslines. Talk about an entrepreneurial spirit! I think I was out about five bucks. Then the store moved into her room because it got cold outside. Whenever friends would come by, Taylor would approach me and say, 'Do you think I could invite them to my store?' So they would go to her store and buy something. She was saving money for her summer vacation. A month later I asked how much she had saved and she said, 'seventy-five dollars.' Then a couple of weekends ago, she decided to have a 'gallery showing,' and wanted me to help her set it up. I said, 'Are you going to charge for this?' She said, 'No, it's really just for people to look and have treats.' I said, 'You mean like a public relations event?' and she said, 'Yes.' She is amazing to me."

MY AUNTIE HAS SHOWN ME ANOTHER WAY TO LIVE

*A*n auntie is often an "other mother," providing another role model of how to live our lives as women. Our mothers, of course, are valuable role models, but sometimes an aunt can provide an alternative style of living. Can you think of ways in which your auntie has shown you a different path?

_____

_____

_____

_____

_____

_____

_____

_____

MY NIECE HAS ADDED ANOTHER DIMENSION TO MY LIFE

Many times, aunties are surprised and delighted to find how much the arrival of a niece, whether born or "adopted" into their world, affects their lives. For women without children, they may realize that they are suddenly an important part of a child's life. For women with children of their own, the new relationship may be a chance for them to be friends with a child without having to be the primary authority figure. Women have described how they can be different people in relationships with nieces. As an aunt, have you seen yourself differently? How has your life changed since your niece came into it?

_____

_____

_____

_____

_____

_____

_____

"I have four adult children, but I think that for me, as an auntie,
I don't feel that terrible weight of responsibility or guilt that I feel with
my own children. That kind of frees me up to be a different person.
It frees me up to be myself."

—Eileen

PHOTO OPPORTUNITIES

*O*n this and the facing page, include photos, mementos, drawings, ticket stubs, or anything else that reminds you of your early years together.

BIRTHDAYS AND HOLIDAYS

*G*ifts, good food, and extra attention—birthdays and holidays provide many opportunities for anticipation and surprise. An auntie often gets as excited about a niece's birthday as her niece does, and her preparations for a holiday are more joyous with a child in mind. If an auntie and a niece live far apart, birthdays and holidays may be the only times of the year they see each other and they try to make these visits memorable. Many women recall special traditions with a niece or aunt around during these celebratory occasions. Do you hold dear any birthday celebrations or holiday moments with a niece or aunt? Do you have a mental image that you treasure? Please record these memories and traditons here in words or in pictures.

Auntie remembers . . .

_____

_____

_____

_____

Niece remembers . . .

_____

_____

_____

_____

Every Year

Karen recalls birthday traditions of many years, "My Auntie Rosie, Auntie
Josephine, and my Auntie Philly never forget birthdays. Every birthday, when
I was growing up, my Auntie Philly would telephone and, in a nasal tone say:
'Western Union calling' and then start singing 'Happy Birthday' to me over
the phone. My Auntie Rosie will send cards. She draws these cute little stick
figures. Her stick figures always have a glass of wine in their right hand. She
writes 'Cheers' or 'Salut' on the bottom of the card. Every year, I will get
cards and my aunts will call. I get phone calls from my Auntie Josephine.
They never forget. Thirty-two years and this has happened since I was old
enough to pick up the phone."

A TRIBUTE TO THE PERSON WHO
BROUGHT US TOGETHER

*E*very aunt and niece who have a close friendship spend time together without other people around, especially as the child gets older. But someone else brought you two together originally, usually a parent who wants an auntie to become part of a niece's life. Many parents are happy to have another loving adult in their children's circle of friends, someone who can provide trusted judgement and a safe haven. Bringing an auntie into the family circle may also have a positive effect on the entire family. Now might be the time to record how that loving person helped your relationship along, and how that relationship has affected the whole family.

The person who encouraged our relationship is . . .

_____

He or she supported our relationship by . . .

_____

_____

_____

How has the relationship affected or helped the rest of your family?

_____

_____

_____

If you have a photo of the three of you together, place it here.
(A drawing will work too!)

Part of Our Family

Ann, now forty-three, tells us about the moment when she realized how important her mother was to the relationship she had with her aunt. "My father died suddenly when he was on vacation. It was unexpected, and it was hard. The whole family—six siblings and their respective families—was at the funeral home. My aunt was there, and she was really part of our family, always a surrogate mother in many ways. As she and I were hugging, with tears streaming down our faces, she said to me, 'You know, I just cannot think enough about your mother. She always allowed me to be such a big part of your family and to be there all the time with you kids. A lot of women would not have let that happen.' It was very touching because my aunt was so important to us, and I had never thought about it from my mother's perspective, about how hard it was to let somebody else into the family to that extent."

THINGS TO HELP US REMEMBER

his page offers an opportunity to add mementos, drawings, or photos that are souvenirs of your relationship.

PART TWO

GOOD TIMES TOGETHER

"My Auntie Josephine, my Auntie Rosie, and my Auntie Philly—
my husband calls them the Greek chorus—they're sisters, always
talking among themselves, always coming up with these grand
ideas. It's this kind of group effort."

–Karen

*N*ieces frequently speak of a time in their lives when an auntie recognized their desires like no one else. Auntie provided piano lessons when parents said no, tucked a longed-for doll or book under the Christmas tree, or arranged an outing that a niece always wanted to take. And aunties got just as excited about the giving as the nieces were about the receiving. One aunt's face lit up as she told us about the pink teepee she had custom-made for an extraordinary birthday gift for her niece! If you are a niece, recall your favorite gift from your auntie and describe why it was so important to you.

I *will always remember* . . .

the way you wrapped . . .

_____

how I felt when you gave me . . .

_____

how everyone envied . . .

_____

If you are an aunt, write about what providing something that fulfilled a child's desire meant to you.

To Jocelyn, with Love

Jocelyn, an opera fan in part because of her auntie's influence, recalls an especially thoughtful gift from her aunt, "When I was a relatively new opera fan, and she knew I was coming to visit her in San Francisco, she stood in line for hours to get an autograph on a record album from Luciano Pavarotti. Hours and hours, and then my aunt stood in line at the opera house and got me the sole available ticket for a sold-out performance of an opera he only performed once. I still have the record jacket and I want to frame it some day, but now it is hidden away among my operas. When I pull it out, it still says, 'To Jocelyn, with love, Luciano Pavarotti'—all in Italian. My aunt has done wonderful things for me. She is pretty great."

TRAVELS WITH AUNTIE

S ometimes aunties and nieces live around the corner from one another, sometimes they live across the country. Often an aunt's physical location provides an exciting opportunity for a niece to travel. An auntie who is an urban dweller can show her niece from a small town what city living is like. We also heard from nieces who found that visiting an auntie who lived in the country, or a remote area, provided a welcome change of pace from their everyday lives in more urban settings. Somehow aunties and nieces manage to stay close regardless of geographical distance. What is your situation? If you live far apart, how do you stay in contact with each other?

Auntie: I live in _____.

Niece: I live in _____.

We live _____ miles apart.

We communicate by _____

_____

Please include a photograph of a visit together.

Sometimes aunties and nieces go on the road together—from spontaneous trips to Disneyland to long-planned vacations to Hawaii or New York. What was it like traveling with auntie? Aunties, what did you most enjoy about the trip with your nieces?

Record your travel remembrances here.

_____

_____

_____

_____

_____

A Map of the United States

Stephanie recalls a special moment with her niece during a trip to her home town. "I remember going over to the grade school that was near my parents' house, and there, painted on the playground, was this gigantic map of the United States. It was probably thirty to forty feet wide. My niece Haley and I were talking, she was about six at the time. She said, 'This is Indiana, right?' And I said, 'You stand right here on it.' Then I said, 'I live here,' as I walked all the way across this map to California. I turned around and looked at her. She got these big tears in her eyes and said, 'Why do you live so far away?' It was with that purity, that beauty, that truth that only a child can deliver. It was a question I still have trouble answering."

You really stood up for me when...

*O*f course, in any meaningful relationship, not all times together are "good." One could argue that no relationship is really solid until we have to defend each other or get involved in each other's troubles. Sometimes we do not realize an auntie is also a friend until she stands up for us at a critical time. Can you recall when your aunt stepped in when you were in trouble?

Write your story here.

_____

_____

_____

_____

_____

_____

_____

_____

_____

_____

_____

_____

_____

Things Are Going to Be Okay

Nancy R., now forty-six, tells how her aunt helped her in a very sticky situation, "In the late sixties, I had just turned eighteen, and my girlfriend and I were going to her boyfriend's apartment to deliver a gift. We drove to the apartment, which he shared with other people. As we were chatting, several plainclothes policemen burst inside. The police officers started questioning us: 'Why are you here? What is in that box?' I said, 'Oh, this is just a gift for our friend.' They ripped it open and sure enough that's all it was. But then they found another box with dope in it. We were lined up, handcuffed, put in the back of a paddy wagon, and taken to jail. It was absolutely traumatic.

"My Aunt Eileen's husband at that time was an attorney, and my aunt and I had always been very, very close. I got Aunt Eileen on the phone and she said, 'Did you do anything?' I said, 'No, I really didn't.' She said, 'Don't worry. We'll get you bailed out.' The story was on the front page of the local paper with our names listed. I came from a very influential family, so my last name was recognizable. Even though the charges against my girlfriend and me had been dropped, my folks were quite upset. It was a very ugly situation. But my aunt was very supportive and said, 'Don't worry, things are going to be okay.' She was the person who stood by my side. When I wanted to talk to someone during this awful period, I would go into another room and make a phone call to my aunt, and say, 'Auntie, it is Nancy. You've got to help me—they are not letting me leave the house.' And she would come to pick me up and take me to lunch. My folks trusted her enough that she was able to spring me from the house. My relationship with my aunt is very special and she is always the person, even to this day, that I call when a difficult family situation arises."

A Helping Hand

Many women of all ages recall a time when an auntie helped in other ways than coming to their defense. Whether dispensing advice, assisting with a school project, or even taking care of us when our parents could not, an aunt frequently comes to the rescue in a child's life. Can you remember a time when your auntie helped out?

Record that story here.

_____

_____

_____

_____

_____

_____

_____

_____

_____

_____

Exactly What I Needed

Ann tells how an auntie helped her see her career situation in a different light and make an important life decision, "Over the years, my aunt has always been a good source of advice as well as being good just to talk to. Last summer, when I was thinking about starting my own business, the most inspirational conversation I had was with her. She held the same administrative job at a telephone company for forty-some years and lived in the same house and took care of my grandmother most of her life. So she had what looked from the outside like a conservative life. I was thinking of leaving my job and starting my own business, and I just remember sitting with her talking about it. She said at one point, 'You just don't know when these chances are going to come, and you might as well try it.' It sounds simple perhaps, but it meant so much coming from my aunt, because it demonstrated not only her belief in me, but also her willingness to encourage me even if it was very different from the way she had lived her life. She was somebody I felt had lived a very straight-ahead life, yet she was saying, 'It's a wonderful thing to own your own business. You should try what you want to try, because that is a good thing.' She offered me perspective when she advised, 'You know, if you are not happy where you are, you need to change that,' which is something I didn't expect her to say. I thought she would say, 'Well, you should really look for something more stable.' She gave me advice that I wasn't expecting. And it was exactly what I needed."

FUN, FUN, FUN!

*F*or every niece with a beloved auntie, there is a day that stands out—an event, great or small, that you remember as being one of the best times of your life. Perhaps it was spontaneous, such as going shopping, baking cookies, or watching movies together. Perhaps it was something you had planned for a long time together, such as giving a party or taking a trip. Whatever it was, neither of you will ever forget it! On this page and the next, write your memories of that time together or add a photograph.

_____

_____

_____

_____

_____

_____

The State Fair

Ruth talks about going to the state fair with her niece, "When Mira got to be about five or six, we decided she was old enough to go, and since then we have been going every year. Two or three years ago, Mira and I stayed all day because they have an agricultural exhibit where farm animals are about to give birth. That day, a cow was in labor, and we *were not* leaving until that calf came. So we spent all day at the fair, from 11 a.m. to eight at night. We were just waiting for that cow to have its calf, which it finally did. Mira thought it was the greatest thing. . . . She was not leaving, she wasn't tired, she wasn't hot, she wasn't distracted! It was pure concentration on this cow and this calf. It didn't bother her that it was really goopy and the little calf had this goo on it. She really enjoyed it. That was a special time."

I Can't Believe My Auntie Did That!

*O*ne of the things we may enjoy most about each other is our ability to do silly or outrageous things around each other. An auntie doesn't have the serious responsibilities of being a parent, who must discipline us and make sure we eat our vegetables. An auntie can get out her old hula-hoop and demonstrate to her niece the technique she refined as a child. Of course, the benefit to auntie is that she can be silly with her niece in a way that she would feel, well, silly about if she were acting that way by herself. What outrageous behavior do you appreciate in your aunt? If you are an auntie, what do you get to do with your niece that you wouldn't do by yourself?

Include stories and photographs on this page and the next.

_____

_____

_____

_____

_____

_____

_____

_____

_____

_____

_____

_____

_____

_____

_____

_____

_____

_____

_____

Queen for a Day

Jolly laughingly recalls her delight when her nieces helped her fulfill a fantasy she had had for years, "I had planned for a couple of years that I was going to celebrate my fiftieth birthday by holding a prom, because I didn't go to the prom in high school. And I was going to be queen. But it had been a terrible year the year I turned fifty, a lot of bad stuff happened, so I just didn't get around to having my prom. I have two nieces who had been queens of the same small town festival in different years. When we got together to celebrate my fiftieth birthday—we happened to be at their parents' house where all their old memorabilia was—they put on two of their crowns and gave me the biggest crown! I have this fabulous photograph of the three of us. I am queen and they are my princesses. It was wonderful—I have a crown, I have a scepter, they have their little tiaras on, I have a bouquet of flowers. It was hysterically funny for us and is one of my favorite memories."

OUR TRADITIONS

$\mathcal{M}$ any aunties and nieces establish traditions—sometimes nonsensical, sometimes serious—just to be shared with each other. Your tradition may be something you do every month, year, birthday, or holiday. Whether it is getting together for that annual holiday shopping trip or a trek into the forest every spring, aunties and nieces find ways to stay connected. What traditions do you have that are unique to your relationship? If you have not yet established a tradition between you, but would like to do so, what would it be?

_____

_____

_____

_____

_____

_____

_____

Ode to a Rutabaga

Jeanette tells about her favorite tradition with her niece, "Although it's a joke between Elaine and me, the whole family laughs about it. The tradition started so many years ago I can't even remember, but it came about because we are Scandinavian and Scandinavians have a dish of mashed-together rutabagas and potatoes. It's disgusting. So years ago I said to my niece, 'If you remember nothing else I tell you, remember never to eat rutabagas.' We laughed about it and that's how our rutabaga tradition started. Over the years we've done different things with rutabagas. One year she gave me a can of them for a gift. Another time I dropped off a rutabaga in a brown paper bag on her doorstep with a poem called 'Ode to Rutabagas.' It was a long, drawn-out poem about what would happen to you if you ate them. Then when she was up for the Aquatenniel Queen of the Lake (a regional goodwill ambassador pageant), the girls were sequestered for a week. We couldn't talk to her, but we could bring her little gifts to let her know we were thinking about her. So my daughters and I decorated a rutabaga, made a crown on it with little jewels, and had it delivered. It was very silly and fun. This rutabaga stuff has been going on for fifteen years."

I Can Tell Her Anything

*L*ike good friends, aunties and nieces often have deep, as well as frivolous, discussions about various aspects of life. As the good friends that they are, they keep each other's secrets. Many nieces told us about a time when they were able to tell their aunties something that they couldn't discuss with anyone else. Parents can be relieved to know that their child has a safe person to talk with about topics too risqué or too scary to discuss with them! Has an auntie ever held a confidence for you? Or helped you sort out a problem you couldn't discuss with anyone else? If you are an aunt, how did you feel when a niece shared a confidence with you?

_____

_____

_____

_____

_____

_____

_____

_____

_____

_____

It's in the Vault

Jolly, now fifty-one, relishes the trust her nieces have shown her, "I have two nieces who are sisters. When she was in college, the older sister trusted me with her secrets. They are her secrets and they will stay secret. The younger sister is quite a bit younger and, as she got a little older to the point where she had secrets, she started talking to her older sister. I found out that the older sister said to the younger sister, 'If you ever need to talk to anybody, talk to Aunt Jolly.' It just made such an impact on me. It is all about loving me and valuing me and trusting me. Those are all the things that are absolutely critical in my life. Every auntie should have such an experience."

YOU HAVE HELPED ME BECOME ME!

$\mathcal{E}$very relationship that is meaningful to a woman affects her in some way. An auntie may help a niece develop her personality, attitudes, or sense of style as a woman. A niece may bring out another aspect of an aunt's character or personality. How has the auntie-and-niece relationship affected you?

_____

_____

_____

_____

_____

_____

_____

_____

_____

_____

_____

_____

_____

A Pell-Mell Life

One woman tells how her auntie was instrumental in establishing her life philosophy, "My Auntie Bobbie was the perfect antimother role model. Probably in my middle school years, I started calling her my Auntie Mame. She is eighty years old now, and she still signs her letters that way.

She is the one who had romances, who had travels, and who had an exotic life. She was not housebound. I'm sure there were sad things about her life, but to me, it was exotic and beautiful and wonderful. Auntie Bobbie had great clothes and she went out for drinks and she did all those things that those glamorous ladies did. I was always welcome at her house in San Francisco as well, which I think is one of the best places in the world. So I would visit there, going by myself when I was in college. But one of my favorite stories about her is when I went to visit her when I was about eleven or twelve years old. We had a lovely chat, spent the whole evening together, and I had my first real drink. She introduced me to vodka gimlets and told me stories about men. It was one of those rites of passage. I had no idea there was a world like that out there. Auntie Bobbie was really wonderful for that. She had a great love for theater and opera. On those many trips to San Francisco, we would usher together at plays and she took me to see all kinds of things. Before I visited her, she would always say, 'Don't forget to bring your black dress,' because in order to usher, you have to wear black. What I learned from her was to live life pell-mell, to go out and embrace life."

IN THAT MOMENT

*O*ne common attribute of the auntie and niece relationship is the level of pride that each generally has in the other. Aunties glowed as they spoke of the intelligence, creativity, beauty, and kindness of their nieces. Nieces reflected on the sophistication, grace, wit, and just general "coolness" of their aunts. But aside from the mutual admiration, often there is a specific memory or story that comes to mind when asked to illustrate our pride in one another. At what moment were you most proud of the other?

_____

_____

_____

_____

_____

_____

_____

_____

_____

_____

_____

Emily

An auntie tells us a story of her sensitive and compassionate niece, "Recently my husband developed a serious illness and I was really frightened. When I spoke to my niece about it, she offered me comforting words. Not just lip service, but really compassionate, intelligent advice that made me feel stronger and more capable of handling the situation. I remember feeling so thankful that she was in my life, for all the joy and love that she has given me. But mostly I felt so proud of my niece who grew from an adorable little baby into a gracious, intelligent, and loving woman. When I introduce her to a friend, I think, 'I am so very proud of the way you are living your life.' My heart is very full when I think of Emily."

A Few of Our Favorite Things

*A*unties and nieces often share similar tastes and enjoy some of the same activities. How do your likes and dislikes match up?

	Auntie's Favorite	*Niece's Favorite*
Comfort food		
TV show		
Book or Author		
Movie		
Ice Cream		
Band		
Perfume		

And, of course, there may be a few things for which you share a mutual dislike.

We have a distinct distaste for . . .

People who _____

Friends who _____

Vegetables that are _____

Boys/men who _____

Magazines that _____

Do you have any "code" for each other—private jokes or nicknames? Record them here (in code, of course!).

_____

_____

_____

_____

A *Culinary Risk*

Karen tells us how her auntie persuaded her to take some culinary risks, "She took me out to my very first French restaurant and ordered escargot. The rule was you just had to try it. If you didn't like it, you didn't have to keep eating it. I said, 'But Auntie Toots, they're snails!' 'No, no, they're escargot. Try one and see if you like it.' To this day, I love escargot."

OUR RELATIONSHIP HAS CHANGED . . .

*A*s we get older, some aspects of our relationship are bound to change. For instance, the excitement of going to buy doughnuts at our favorite bakery or visiting Santa Claus at the local mall at Christmas time may fade. Instead, we may start wearing the same size of clothing and can borrow each other's stuff. Going clothes shopping together becomes a fun outing instead of a chore. How has your relationship changed over the years?

_____

_____

_____

_____

_____

_____

*A*lthough what we do together may shift over time, the bonds that hold us together, the mesh of our personalities, the honesty and support we give each other, may not ever change. How has your relationship been consistent over your history together?

_____

_____

_____

_____

_____

_____

_____

A Turning Point

*M*any nieces remember a critical moment in their lives when an auntie assisted them, perhaps when a parent was unavailable or unable to help. This often happens when a girl or young woman is wrestling with feelings or situations that she may be too young to understand yet herself. Can you think of a time when an auntie has helped you sort out your feelings? Perhaps an auntie has helped you make a crucial decision in your life. Can you recall such a time?

If so, record it here.

_____

_____

_____

_____

_____

_____

_____

_____

A Beautiful Little Maple

Amber, a twenty-one-year-old niece, talks about how her auntie helped her find closure after the death of her father, "My parents divorced when I was nine and I didn't see my father again until I was fifteen, the same year he passed away. It was difficult not seeing him, but my auntie helped me tremendously during that time. She encouraged me to talk and share my feelings (without being obtrusive), and she always listened with an open heart. One thing I always wanted to do was find a way to commemorate him. It was always on my mind, but for some reason I couldn't take the steps to do it. My auntie kept reminding me gently to do it, to find closure. Over the course of four or five years, she kept bringing it up, saying, 'What would you like to do for your dad?' Initially, I had wanted to plant a tree in his honor, but was uncertain about how to proceed. My auntie reminded me periodically, mentioning a local park as a possibility. She wasn't pushing me, she just said, 'It might be a nice idea, and if you want me to look into it, I'd be more than happy to do so.'

"Finally, she and I and my brother bought a tree, went to a park, and planted a beautiful little maple for my dad. I couldn't have done it without her. Since I was away at college, she made all the arrangements. My auntie called me and asked, 'What kind of tree would you like?' She ordered the tree, talked to the ranger, arranged the time, met me and my brother, and we went with the ranger and watched him plant and put a fence around it.

"And my auntie is still helping me honor my father. Recently, she said, 'Would you like to go see how the tree is doing?' So we went back to the tree, pulled all the weeds around it, watered it, and plucked off its dead leaves. It was a really special thing that she made this effort and I felt really close with her when we did that together.

"She was really the bridge between me and my dad—even when he was alive. She was never on one side or the other when my parents divorced. My aunt was very supportive of my dad and of my mother, and very supportive of me. She has never taken sides, even now."

Looking Back

*U*se this page to include objects and photos that remind you of past experiences—vacations, holidays, birthdays, outings—which you have shared.

PART THREE
LOOKING AHEAD

"I sometimes think that our connection was meant to be,

because she is just the most extraordinary human being—

I don't even mean as a two year old. I just mean as a human being.

My niece brought the whole family together, and now I have

a new person to take places, I have a new person to buy gifts for, I have a new

person to call on the phone. It's a new connection, and it's just great."

—Miriam

WHEN THE TIME IS RIGHT

*E*veryone is short on time, right? Even when you are an eight year old, your schedule may be filled with Girl Scouts, dance lessons, sleepover parties, and other rites of passage. Chances are the amount of time you can spend with your auntie becomes less and less as you grow older. If you are a grown-up aunt, you know this problem as well. Life just seems to get busier and busier! So if you two do not get to spend much time with each other now, start planning the things you would like to do together in the future.

_____

_____

_____

_____

_____

_____

_____

_____

_____

_____

_____

Looking to the Future

One woman gleefully reveals her anticipation of spending more time with her niece, "Since my niece was born, we have lived at least two thousand miles apart. Now that she is sixteen, she is talking about where she is going to go to college and where she will live after graduation. She has been telling her mother that she wants to eventually live on the West Coast where I now live. Her mother and I joke around all the time, her mother warning me not to support this notion, and me—with my fingers crossed behind me—solemnly swearing that I would never encourage my niece's wish to move West. Of course, I would love it, and I can imagine my niece enjoying the area where I live, just like I do. I would love to have her here, close to me physically as well as emotionally."

SOMETHING TO PASS ALONG

*O*ne of the greatest gifts an aunt can give a niece is a sense of how the niece fits into the history of her family and the world. This sense can allow our nieces the opportunity to see themselves as part of the tapestry of a family, a friendship, a generation, a culture.

Each woman carries personal memories of her family, and remembrances specific to her generation. We all know how a particular phrase or conversation, a specific afternoon or event, can stick with us forever. Unless an auntie passes those memories on to the next generation, many of those impressions and stories will be lost. If you are an auntie, please record here anything you wish your niece to know and remember about her family, your childhood or lessons of your generation. These can be broad observations—common experiences of members of your generation, or stories and memories specific to your own life. It may be a photograph of a grandmother that your niece has never met, a newspaper clipping of an important event in your life, or a recipe that you wish to pass on to your niece—whatever information you hope is never lost.

_____

_____

_____

_____

_____

WHAT I WISH FOR YOU . . .

*O*ne of the best things about having a close relationship with an auntie or niece is sharing the journey of life together. Of course, we want our niece or aunt to get what they want out of life, as well as enjoying themselves, appreciating learning, and experiencing love. As we look forward, there are hopes and dreams we have for one another. What do you wish for each other as you envision the future?

Write them here so you can share them.

_____

_____

_____

_____

_____

_____

_____

_____

_____

_____

_____

_____

What About the Monsters?

Eileen, also known as Mimi by her godchild, tells us of one of her favorite memories, "She always asks me when I see her, 'Mimi, tell me the things that you will save me from.' So we go through a little ritual, like 'Oh, if you ever go to jail, I'll come to jail and get you out;' 'If the bad guys ever come, I'll come after you;' or 'If a dog chases you down the street, I'll find you and save you,' and such things. My godchild loves these little stories and then she always says, 'Now what about monsters? Will you save me from the monsters, too?' I say, 'Sure, just call me up.' It is so sweet."

WORDS TO LIVE BY

*L*ife has its ups and downs. Sometimes the only things that get us through the "down" periods are encouraging words lovingly expressed. What would you like to say to your auntie or your niece in times of confusion, trouble, or just when they need a little extra boost?

Write them here so you both will have them forever.

_____

_____

_____

_____

_____

_____

_____

_____

_____

Remember Who Loves You

When asked what she would want her niece to always keep in mind, Stephanie responded, "Remember where you came from and remember who loves you. And remember, no matter what happens to you, *that* is the core of who you are. If you look over the first years of your life at home, the landscape is littered with really good people who love you to death. In the times that will lie ahead, and in the times when your heart is hurting and you feel like no one in the world understands you—that maybe you are a mess—you can't wipe out where you came from and who loves you. That counts, not just for something, but for almost everything.

THE NEXT GENERATION

*Y*ou nieces have benefited from the love, care, daring, and opinions of your aunties. Do you have a niece of your own? Who is your niece? Is she in your family or do you look forward to adopting one? What have you received from your auntie that you wish to pass on to your niece?

_____

_____

_____

_____

_____

If you already have a niece and a picture of her, include it here.

If the "next generation" niece is old enough, ask her to draw a picture of the three of you here.

A Woman's Circle

"Mary broadened my horizons, made my world a bigger place. I've told her many times, 'I don't know, Mary, if you will ever know what an effect you have had on my life.' I told her I could never repay her. Her response has been always, 'Nancy, you can repay me by doing the same thing for someone else someday.' At forty years old, I truly understand what that means. After immersing myself in an eating disorder for practically twenty years, I have stepped out of the chaos with a greater awareness of what I have to offer. It's very exciting to be at this point in my life where I can do for other kids what she has done for me. It's so incredible to see this circle, this cycle, really coming to pass."

Thank You

Even if we know we love each other, we sometimes may not know how much we are appreciated in the other's life. Putting those feelings into words or on paper can have a powerful effect. Is there anything you would like to say to each other? A thank you that has not yet been said (or at least not recorded)?

_____

_____

_____

_____

_____

_____

_____

_____

_____

_____

_____

A Valuable Lesson

One woman, now fifty-one years old, describes how she let her auntie know how much she appreciated her influence, "Probably the most important thing I did as an adult in connection with my aunt was when I was about forty-five years old. What I learned from her was to 'go for the gusto,' to not be intimidated by experience. It was an Auntie Mame kind of thing, 'go out and embrace life'—that was a really valuable lesson from her. I wrote to thank her and tell her it was wonderful that there was a woman out there, who was not my mother, to show me that there were different things that women could do in life, who would listen to me, and do all those things that aunties do. I wrote her a letter telling her how much I appreciated her having played that role in my life. I thanked her for all of her kindness and love."

As her voice trembled with emotion, this devoted niece continued, "Writing that letter continues to be one of the most important things I ever did for her. She thinks about it, she talks about it. She is really proud of that letter. But you know, it was a gift for me to do that. I needed to do it."

Your Connection Forever

*U*se these pages to ensure that your keepsake book is up to date! Include pictures, ticket stubs, programs, drawings, and anything else you can attach to the page to memorialize your shared experiences.